Python Practical Guide

RIPAL RANPARA

Table of Contents

ACKNOWLEDGMENTS

I offer my prayers and gratitude in the lotus feet of my Guru H.D.H. Hariprasad Swamiji Maharaj for his blessings and guidance.

I would like to thank the Honorable Secretary P.P. Sadhu Tyagvallabhdas of Yogidham Gurukul, whose blessings and best wishes were with me in this academic endeavour.

I also take this opportunity to thank the Principal Shree M & N Virani Science College Dr. K. D. Ladva for their support and motivation.

I place on record, my sincere gratitude to Dr.Stavan Patel & Dr. Hitendra Donga. HOD Department of Computer Science & IT, for constant support and encouragement.

I would like to offer my sincere gratitude to my role model Dr.Sheetal Tank ; for her constant support in my research work. I thank her for her patience, motivation, methodology, and the immense knowledge of the field of research study.

I take this opportunity to record our sincere thanks to all the faculty members of the Department of Computer Science & IT for their help and encouragement. I also thank my parents for their unceasing encouragement and support. I also place on record, my sense of gratitude to one and all who, directly or indirectly, have lent their helping hand in this journey.

1 INTRODUCTION TO PYTHON

What Is Python?

Python is an interpreted object-oriented language that is available on multiple platforms (hardware systems) and multiple operating systems (software systems). You can take the same Python script file and run it on Microsoft Windows™, Apple Macintosh™, Unix™, or a dozen other potential platforms that the language has been implemented for. The language itself is a standard, so any valid Python script will run, unmodified, on any platform that supports the interpreter.

Python is an extensible language, meaning that you can add to it with your own source code, modules, and components that can then be reused in other applications. Python is a small language, meaning that it has a tiny memory "footprint," and, in fact, is used in many handheld devices for programming.

Python is one of the foundations of LAMP (or WAMP) application development. LAMP stands for the four pillars of the open source community, Linux, Apache, MySQL, and Python (or PHP). Python gives you the capability to interface to databases, to create CGI scripts that can be run from a Web browser, to create applications that can be run in a Windows environment, and to create extensible scripts that function in the business or scientific world. Python has been used in everything from business Web sites to online games, from simple conversion scripts to complex Internet update routines for banks and other financial institutions.

A Brief History of Python

In the late 1980s, in the Netherlands, a programmer named Guido van Rossum, then working at CWI (the National Research Institute for Mathematics and Computer Science in the Netherlands) was working with a language called ABC on a platform called the Amoeba operating system. Amoeba was an experimental, microkernel-based distributed operating system developed by Andrew S. Tanenbaum and others at the Vrije University.

The aim of the Amoeba project was to build a timesharing system that made an entire network of computers appear to the user as a single machine. Mr. Van Rossum liked the language a lot, but recognized that   it had a number of shortcomings.

The basis for the Python language was ABC, which was very similar to BASIC or Pascal. It was an excellent teaching language, did not require variable declarations, and used indentation for nesting of statements. These bits of functionality, you will find, are core to the Python implementation as well. While ABC was more of a monolithic language that tended to produce large, hard-to-debug applications, Python was designed more to be object-oriented and modular.

The really exciting changes to Python came after van Rossum's work at CWI was complete. He and his team of programmers had moved from CWI to the BeOpen labs. This open-structured programming laboratory led the team to explore new directions for the language. In the great tradition of all programming tasks, the team "borrowed" from other languages to extend their own. Much in the same was that the C language borrowed constructs from previous languages such as Pascal or FORTRAN, Python 2.0 borrowed from a language called Haskell. The biggest change for Python came in the release that was centered around the second major version. Python had become a standard language, with a group responsible for its development and for approving all enhancements to the language standard.

The Python Software Foundation was created. This board used a standard method, called the Python Enhancement Proposal (PEP), to offer up to the programming community suggestions for new language enhancements. These enhancements have been gathered and streamlined and will become Python 3.0 when it becomes available. The biggest change for the third major release will be the first break with backward compatibility to fix perceived errors in the language. Whether or not this will actually happen is still in debate. In any case, the future of Python is quite rosy, and the spirited debate on its functionality and future ensure that it will be around for a long time to come.

Interpreters Versus Compilers

The first thing that is important to understand about Python is that it is an interpreted language. There are two sorts of programming languages: interpreted ones and compiled ones. A compiled language is what you are probably used to if you have done any programming in the past. The
process for a compiled language is as follows:

Create source file using text edit→
Use compiler to syntax check and convert source file into binary →
Use linker to turn binary files into executable format→
Run the resulting executable format file in the operating system.

The biggest difference between interpreted code and compiled code is that an interpreted application need not be "complete." You can test it in bits and pieces until you are satisfied with the results and put them all together later for the end user to use.

Note: When to Use (or Not Use) an Interpreted Language

As with any approach to a problem, there are advantages and disadvantages to using an interpreted language. Let's take a look at some of these, so you can get a sense of the balance you need to use in determining when a language such as Python makes sense, and when it does not.

Advantages

1. Easier to debug and maintain the code.
2. Easier to update the application code quickly.
3. Errors can be fixed quickly without the need for complete redistribution
4. Can be embedded in other languages.

Disadvantages

1. You need to do more things to the end user.
2. The source files can be modified by the end user
3. Errors aren't found until runtime.

Understanding Bytecodes

As mentioned previously, Python uses "bytecodes" to actually do the work of processing the source code. The bytecode idea is not new, as there are quite a number of languages that use something similar. The idea is that a statement is broken down into a "code," indicating what it is going to do, and then a series of arguments to that code. For example, you might have something like this:

```
print value1
```

The "code" for print might be 0x01 (it doesn't really matter what the value is). The argument to the print statement is a value. So, in the byte code version of the source code, you might see something like this:

```
<0x01><value><end-of-statement>
```

When the interpreter loads the bytecode version of the file, it reads a code and recognizes it as a print statement. The interpreter then knows to read in arguments until the end of statement marker is encountered. This is quite different from the compiled version of the program, where the statement is literally turned into a series of machine statements that the native operating system can process.

Why Use Python?

Object-Oriented
Python is an object-oriented language. Most existing interpreted and scripting languages are simple line-oriented, sequential languages, which indicates that reuse is virtually impossible and debugging and maintaining the code is difficult. Python is a structured language constructed around classes and reusable components called modules. This allows you to easily move your Python code from project to project, saving you enormous amounts of time.

Cross Platform
Python code is written in Python itself, so any platform that will run the interpreter will run them. This allows you to move forward knowing that no matter what changes the company you work for decides to make with respect to hardware and software, your Python code is going to work like a champ. This particular attribute is one of the main reasons that so much Internet code is written in Python, because it makes it easy to port it from server to server.

Well Supported in Third-Party Tools
When you are trying to implement a new application, it is good to know if the existing third-party tools out there will help you out. Python is well supported in such third-party tools as MySQL, an open-source database package, and Apache, an open-source Web server. These are two of the most popular packages for using scripting tools with, and as such, using a well-supported scripting tool is a definite bonus.

In addition to being used by third-party tools, Python can be embedded in other applications. There are a number of examples of this, which makes it easier to convince other people to use Python rather than a less supported engine.

Good Selection of Tools Available

Python comes with an excellent set of pre-built tools, for which source code is available. This makes it easier to develop high-quality code, which in turn makes it easier to worry about your application features and not about whether or not your system is going to crash the first time someone uses it.

Good Selection of Pre-built Libraries

As mentioned previously, Python lends itself well to developing reusable code because of its object-oriented approach to development. This means that there is a lot of already developed code out there that you can reuse. Many of these classes are of general-purpose functionality that you will probably need in your own applications. Email, complex math, and collections are but a few of the libraries that you can easily import into your own applications.

Remember, the less time you spend developing code that the user never sees, the more time you can spend creating functionality that the user really wants. When all is said and done, that is what it is all about, from the perspective of management anyway.

Where Is Python Used?

Here is just a small group of areas in which Python has found itself utilized to make the world a better place:
- Cinematography
- Sports
- Clothing
- Aviation
- Business information
- Document management

- Pharmaceuticals.
- Education
- Government
- Public safety
- Biology
- Chemistry
- Weather
- GIS
- Marine
- Engineering.
- Web pages
- Application development tools

this is only a small fraction of the places in which you will find Python code, so it's likely that your application space has already been used in the past and that code exists to do the more common things you might need.

Installing Python 3 for Windows

To download the Python exe, **visit www.python.org/download/** and download the Python MSI file. Please make sure that you choose the right version concerning your platform. The Python installation may need an administrator account.

For all the stages of the Python installation, you can leave all the settings at their default values. If the installation has been done properly, you should see the following dialog window open:

Figure 1.1 Python Installer.

Installing setup-tools

PIP is a dependence of setuptools. We need to install setuptools to use PIP. The following sections describe how we can install setuptools on windows operating systems.

To download the setuptools executable, you have to go to the PyPI website at https://pypi.python.org/pypi/setuptools. Then, we need to click on Downloads and select the right version. In this book, we use Version 1.1, as shown in the following screenshot:

```
C:\Python33>python.exe c:\Python_extensions\setuptools-1.4b1\setup.py install
```

Python Language Overview

In order to really understand a language, you need to know the components that make up that language. In the case of a programming language, the elements that make up the language are its syntax, its keywords, and the style with which the language expresses itself. To begin with, let's take a simple look at some Python code. Since Python is an interpreted language, there is really no need for the usual start and end blocks; you can simply select the pieces that you want to run and type them into the interpreter. We will be using the IDLE interpreter.

To start up IDLE, just select it from the Start menu in windows (Start Menu | All Programs | Python 2.5 | IDLE (Python GUI)), or run pythonw.exe from the directory in which you installed Python. When you bring up the IDLE editor, it will look like the image shown in Figure 1.2. IDLE, of course, comes from the name of one of the Monty Python actors, Eric Idle.

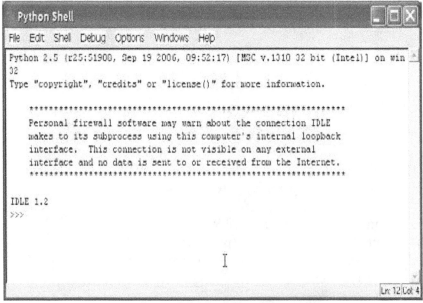

Figure 1.2 The idle editor.

Python syntax

Let's take a closer look at what the actual syntax of python looks Like and what the rules are for using that syntax.

Comments

When you are writing code, it is often useful to place a comment in place to indicate what you are doing. This is particularly useful if you want someone else to be able to ever read your code. The Python language supports comments, using the hash (#) character. The hash character indicates that everything from that point on to the end of the line is a comment. For example, you can use it as a line unto itself:

```
# this is a comment.
```

Alternatively, you can use the comment character at the end of a line of code:

```
X = 1 # initialize x to be the first element.
```

In either case, the text following the comment character is ignored by the interpreter when it is reading and processing the code.

Indentation

If you are accustomed to programming in another language, such as Pascal, C++, or Java, you may be used to the idea of statement termination. For example, in C++, if you want to assign the value 12 to a variable named a, you would write a statement that looks something like this:

```
a = 12;
```

The variable name is a, the action you are taking is "assignment" (using the = operator), and The value you are assigning to the variable is 12. The compiler knows that the statement is Finished when it encounters the end-of-statement token, which in C++ is the semi-colon (;). Likewise, in pascal, you might write something like this:

```
a := 12;
```

Once again, the statement has a variable, an operator (in this case :=
which is the Pascal version Of the C++ operator=), and a value. The
statement is terminated by a semi-colon. Older languages, Such as
FORTRAN, use a different scheme to indicate the end of a
statement. In order To terminate a statement, you use the carriage
return to indicate that the statement is finished. Python, which aims
for simplicity in all things it does, uses a combination of indentation
and End-of-line characters (carriage returns) to indicate statements.
So an assignment in Python looks like this:

```
a = 12
```

That certainly seems simple enough, but what do you do when your
line is too long for a single line of code? For example, suppose that
you want to assign a really long string to a given variable. You might
do something like this:

```
s = "This is a really, really long string that
should not be this long, but it is. How long do
you think it will get before it does something
bad?"
```

As you can tell, the above line is too long to appear on a single line in
the interpreter. Wrapping Text is a bad idea in any language, since the
editor often inserts some sort of carriage return Character to mark a
line wrap. That character inserted indicates to the interpreter that the
Statement ends. So the python interpreter would read the above
statement as:

```
s = "This is a really, really long string that should not
be this long, but it is. How long do you think it will
```

And then follow that with the statement:

```
Get before it does something bad?"
```

The first statement is an error because it does not terminate the literal
string with a closing Double quote. The second statement is an error
because, well, it isn't a statement at all! So, how Do you get around

this little problem? Fortunately, python provides a solution, the line continuation Character. You can write the above as:

```
s = "This is a really, really long string that
should not be this long, but it is. How long do
you think" \ "  it will get before it does
something bad?"
```

Another thing Python provides no braces to indicate blocks of code for class and function definitions or flow control. Blocks of code are denoted by line indentation, which is rigidly enforced.

The number of spaces in the indentation is variable, but all statements within the block must be indented the same amount. For example –

```
if True:
    print "True"
else:
  print "False"
```

However, the following block generates an error –

```
if True:
    print "Answer"
    print "True"
else:
    print "Answer"
  print "False"
```

Thus, in python all the continuous lines indented with same number of spaces would form a block. The following example has various statement blocks –

Note: do not try to understand the logic at this point of time. Just make sure you understood various blocks even if they are without braces.

Multi-Line Statements

Statements in python typically end with a new line. Python does, however, allow the use of the line continuation character (\) to denote that the line should continue. For example −

```
total = item_one + \
        item_two + \
        item_three
```

Statements contained within the [], {}, or () brackets do not need to use the line continuation character. For example −

```
days = ['Monday', 'Tuesday', 'Wednesday',
        'Thursday', 'Friday']
```

Quotation in Python

Python accepts single ('), double (") and triple (''' or """) quotes to denote string literals, as long as the same type of quote starts and ends the string. The triple quotes are used to span the string across multiple lines. For example, all the following are legal −

```
word = 'word'
sentence = "This is a sentence."
paragraph = """This is a paragraph. It is
made up of multiple lines and sentences."""
```

Multiple Statements on a Single Line

The semicolon (;) allows multiple statements on the single line given that neither statement starts a new code block. Here is a sample snip using the semicolon −

```
import sys; x = 'foo'; sys.stdout.write(x + '\n')
```

Python Reserved Words

A keyword is one that means something to the language. In other words, you can't use a reserved word as the name of a variable, a function, a class, or a module. All the Python keywords contain lowercase letters only.

and	exec	not
assert	finally	or
break	for	pass
class	from	print
continue	global	raise
def	if	return
del	import	try
elif	in	while
else	is	with
except	lambda	yield

Hello, world Program

Using the interactive help

Whether you're in IDLE or at a standard interactive prompt, there are a couple of handy tools to help you explore Python. The first is the help() function, which has two modes. You can just enter help() at the prompt to enter the help system, where you can get help on modules, keywords, or topics. When you're in the help system, you see a help> prompt, and you can enter a module name, such as math or some other topic, to browse Python's documentation on that topic. Usually it's more convenient to use help() in a more targeted way. Entering a type or variable name as a parameter for help() gives you an immediate display of that type's documentation:

```
>>> x = 2
>>> help(x)
Help on int object:
class int(object)
 | int(x[, base]) -> integer
```

Convert a string or number to an integer, if possible. A floating point argument will be truncated towards zero (this does not include a string representation of a floating point number!) When converting | string, use the optional base. It is an error to supply a base when converting a non-string. Methods defined here:(continues with a list of methods for an int)

Using help() in this way is handy for checking the exact syntax of a method or the behavior of an object. The help() function is part of the pydoc library, which has several options for accessing the documentation built into Python libraries. Because every Python installation comes with complete documentation, you can have all of the official documentation at your fingertips, even if you aren't online. See the appendix for more information on accessing Python's documentation.

Datatypes

Like most programming languages, Python is made up of building blocks called types. These types define the kinds of data that you can reference in the system and how you can manipulate that data. As with most languages, there are restrictions in Python on what sorts of information you can refer to various data types. Rather than data storage spaces, which is what variables are in most languages, Python uses data references for variables. This means that a variable "refers to" a given piece of data in memory. Unlike many languages, however, Python is not a strongly typed language.

Numeric Types

The first type is the numeric type. Python supports two basic numeric types: integers and floating point numbers.

1.Integers

Integers are whole numbers having a range that depends upon the hardware upon which Python is running. You can have negative integers, positive integers, and zero, which is neither negative or positive. Integers support the full range of arithmetic operations: adding, multiplying, dividing, and subtracting.

Number objects are created when you assign a value to them. For example −

```
var1 = 1
var2 = 10
```

You can also delete the reference to a number object by using the **del** statement. The syntax of the del statement is −

```
del var1[,var2[,var3[....,varN]]]
```

You can delete a single object or multiple objects by using the **del** statement. For example:

```
del var
del var_a, var_b
```

Python supports four different numerical types −

int (signed integers)

They are often called just integers or ints, are positive or negative whole numbers with no decimal point.

long (long integers)

Also called longs, they are integers of unlimited size, written like integers and followed by an uppercase or lowercase L.

float (floating point real values)

Also called floats, they represent real numbers and are written with a decimal point dividing the integer and fractional parts. Floats may also be in scientific notation, with E or e indicating the power of 10 ($2.5e2 = 2.5 \times 10^2 = 250$).

complex (complex numbers)

are of the form a + bJ, where a and b are floats and J (or j) represents the square root of -1 (which is an imaginary number). The real part of the number is a, and the imaginary part is b. Complex numbers are not used much in Python programming.

Examples

int	long	float	complex
10	51924361L	0.0	3.14j
100	-0x19323L	15.20	45.j
-786	0122L	-21.9	9.322e-36j
080	0xDEFABCECBDAECBFBAEL	32.3+e18	.876j
-0490	535633629843L	-90.	-.6545+0J
-0x260	-052318172735L	-32.54e100	3e+26J
0x69	-4721885298529L	70.2-E12	4.53e-7j

Python allows you to use a lowercase L with long, but it is recommended that you use only an uppercase L to avoid confusion with the number 1.

Python displays long integers with an uppercase L.A complex number consists of an ordered pair of real floating point numbers denoted by a + bj, where a is the real part and b is the imaginary part of the complex number.

Number Type Conversion

Python converts numbers internally in an expression containing mixed types to a common type for evaluation. But sometimes, you need to coerce a number explicitly from one type to another to satisfy the requirements of an operator or function parameter.

Type **int(x)** to convert x to a plain integer.

Type **long(x)** to convert x to a long integer.

Type **float(x)** to convert x to a floating-point number.

Type **complex(x)** to convert x to a complex number with real part x and imaginary part zero.

Type **complex(x, y)** to convert x and y to a complex number with real part x and imaginary part y. x and y are numeric expressions

Strings

Python provides a rich array of functionality dedicated toward working with strings.

Enclosed in Quotes

The most obvious way you would work with a string is to place something in quotation marks. For example:

```
name = "My name is Atmiya"
```

This creates a variable called name, which refers to the string literal "My name is Atmiya." You can use either single or double quotation marks to create a string in Python:

Accessing Values in String

Python does not support a character type; these are treated as strings of length one, thus also considered a substring. To access substrings, use the square brackets for slicing along with the index or indices to obtain your substring. For example −

```
var1 = 'Hello World!'
var2 = "Python Programming"

print "var1[0]: ", var1[0]
print "var2[1:5]: ", var2[1:5]
```

When the above code is executed, it produces the following result −

```
var1[0]:  H
var2[1:5]:  ytho
```

Updating Strings

You can "update" an existing string by (re)assigning a variable to another string. The new value can be related to its previous value or to a completely different string altogether. For example −

```
var1 = 'Hello World!'
print "Updated String :- ", var1[:6] + 'Python'
```

When the above code is executed, it produces the following result −

```
Updated String :-  Hello Python
```

Concatenating Strings

After storing and printing, the most utilized function of strings is concatenating, or combining, them into longer strings.

```
output = "The answer is: "
# Decide what the answer should be...
```

```
output += "green"
print output
```

In the above little piece of code, the final result printed would be:

```
The answer is: green
```

Repeating Strings

Python does contain a unique operator in all of the programming languages. The times operator "*," when applied to strings, allows you to repeat a string some number of times. For example:

```
>>> a = "Hello"
>>> a += 5*"there"
>>> print a
Hellotheretheretheretherethere
```

String Special Operators

Assume string variable **a** holds 'Hello' and variable **b** holds 'Python', then –

Operator	Description	Example
+	Concatenation - Adds values on either side of the operator	a + b will give HelloPython
*	Repetition - Creates new strings, concatenating multiple copies of the same string	a*2 will give -HelloHello
[]	Slice - Gives the character from the given index	a[1] will give e
[:]	Range Slice - Gives the characters from the given range	a[1:4] will give ell
in	Membership - Returns true if a character exists in	H in a will give 1

	the given string	
not in	Membership - Returns true if a character does not exist in the given string	M not in a will give 1
r/R	Raw String - Suppresses actual meaning of Escape characters. The syntax for raw strings is exactly the same as for normal strings with the exception of the raw string operator, the letter "r," which precedes the quotation marks. The "r" can be lowercase (r) or uppercase (R) and must be placed immediately preceding the first quote mark.	print r'\n' prints \n and print R'\n'prints \n
%	Format - Performs String formatting	See at next section

String Formatting Operator

One of Python's coolest features is the string format operator %. This operator is unique to strings and makes up for the pack of having functions from C's printf() family. Following is a simple example –

```
print "My name is %s and weight is %d kg!" %
('Abc', 21)
```

When the above code is executed, it produces the following result –

```
My name is Abc and weight is 21 kg!
```
Here is the list of complete set of symbols which can be used along with % –

Format Symbol	Conversion
%c	character
%s	string conversion via str() prior to formatting
%i	signed decimal integer
%d	signed decimal integer
%u	unsigned decimal integer
%o	octal integer
%x	hexadecimal integer (lowercase letters)
%X	hexadecimal integer (UPPERcase letters)
%e	exponential notation (with lowercase 'e')
%E	exponential notation (with UPPERcase 'E')
%f	floating point real number
%g	the shorter of %f and %e
%G	the shorter of %f and %E

String Slicing

A variant of the single index access is multiple index accessing of strings, or slicing of strings. This is done by providing a range of characters that you want. For example, you might want the characters from position three through position eight in the string Hello world. In Python, this is done by using the slicing syntax [3:8]. In fact, if you look at the result of this operation:

```
>>> s[3:8]
'lo wor'
```

You can see that you get exactly what you'd expect. In a range operation, unlike a single character operation, giving numbers outside the bounds of the string is okay. So, you can look at, for example, characters four through 100:

```
>>> s[4:100]
'o world'
```

Formatting Method

Python provides three string methods in the string module for justification, whether you need things right or left justified, or centered within a block.

ljust :Left justify a string within a given width
rjust :Right justify a string within a given width
center :Center a string within a given width.

The functions should be somewhat self-explanatory, but let's give a simple example of how to use them anyway, just in case you might have some question about them.

```
>>> s = "1234"
>>> print s.ljust(10)
1234
>>> print s.rjust(10)
      1234
>>> print s.center(10)
1234
```

Sequences

Sequences in Python are collections of data, shown in various forms. The three specific forms that make up all of the other types in Python are: **Lists, tuples, dictionaries**

They are roughly equivalent to various types of arrays in other languages, but in Python they have special meanings. Let's look at each one of them so that you can understand how they work, what they look like, and how you can use them in your own Python programs.

Python Lists

a list is simply a collection of ordered objects, although the objects need not be of the same type. The list is a most versatile datatype available in Python which can be written as a list of comma-separated values (items) between square brackets. Important thing about a list is that items in a list need not be of the same type.

Creating a list is as simple as putting different comma-separated values between square brackets. For example –

```
list1 = ['physics', 'chemistry', 1997, 2000];
list2 = [1, 2, 3, 4, 5 ];
list3 = ["a", "b", "c", "d"]
```

Similar to string indices, list indices start at 0, and lists can be sliced, concatenated and so on.

Accessing Values in Lists
To access values in lists, use the square brackets for slicing along with the index or indices to obtain value available at that index. For example –

```
list1 = ['physics', 'chemistry', 1997, 2000];
list2 = [1, 2, 3, 4, 5, 6, 7 ];

print "list1[0]: ", list1[0]
print "list2[1:5]: ", list2[1:5]
```

When the above code is executed, it produces the following result –

```
list1[0]:  physics
list2[1:5]:  [2, 3, 4, 5]
```

Updating Lists

You can update single or multiple elements of lists by giving the slice on the left-hand side of the assignment operator, and you can add to elements in a list with the append() method. For example –

```
print "Value available at index 2 : "
print list[2]
list[2] = 2001;
print "New value available at index 2 : "
print list[2]
```

Note: append() method is discussed in subsequent section. When the above code is executed, it produces the following result –

```
Value available at index 2 :
1997
New value available at index 2 :
2001
```

Delete List Elements

To remove a list element, you can use either the del statement if you know exactly which element(s) you are deleting or the remove() method if you do not know. For example –

```
list1 = ['physics', 'chemistry', 1997, 2000];
print list1
del list1[2];
print "After deleting value at index 2 : "
print list1
```

When the above code is executed, it produces following result –

> ['physics', 'chemistry', 1997, 2000]
> After deleting value at index 2 :
> ['physics', 'chemistry', 2000]

Note: remove() method is discussed in subsequent section.

Basic List Operations

Lists respond to the + and * operators much like strings; they mean concatenation and repetition here too, except that the result is a new list, not a string. In fact, lists respond to all of the general sequence operations we used on strings in the prior chapter.

Python Expression	Results	Description
len([1, 2, 3])	3	Length
[1, 2, 3] + [4, 5, 6]	[1, 2, 3, 4, 5, 6]	Concatenation

['Hi!'] * 4	['Hi!', 'Hi!', 'Hi!', 'Hi!']	Repetition
3 in [1, 2, 3]	True	Membership
for x in [1, 2, 3]: print x,	1 2 3	Iteration

Built-in List Functions & Methods:

SN	Function with Description
1	cmp(list1, list2) Compares elements of both lists.
2	len(list) Gives the total length of the list.
3	max(list) Returns item from the list with max value.
4	min(list) Returns item from the list with min value.
5	list(seq) Converts a tuple into list.

Tuples

Once you understand lists, understanding tuples is easy. A tuple is just like a list, except that it is irreversible. In short, you can create a tuple, and iterate over it, but you can't modify the contents of the tuple after it has been created. A tuple is created using a similar syntax as a list:

aTuple = (1, 2.15, "This is a test")

You can print them out:

>>> print aTuple
(1, 2.1499999999999999, 'This is a test')

Note that the floating point value, being stored as a "true" float, will be displayed as an approximation.

Accessing Values in Tuples:

To access values in tuple, use the square brackets for slicing along with the index or indices to obtain value available at that index. For example-

```
tup1 = ('physics', 'chemistry', 1997, 2000);
tup2 = (1, 2, 3, 4, 5, 6, 7 );

print "tup1[0]: ", tup1[0]
print "tup2[1:5]: ", tup2[1:5]
```

When the above code is executed, it produces the following result −

```
tup1[0]:  physics
tup2[1:5]:  [2, 3, 4, 5]
```

Updating Tuples

Tuples are immutable which means you cannot update or change the values of tuple elements. You are able to take portions of existing tuples to create new tuples as the following example demonstrates

```
tup1 = (12, 34.56);
tup2 = ('abc', 'xyz');

# Following action is not valid for tuples
# tup1[0] = 100;

# So let's create a new tuple as follows
tup3 = tup1 + tup2;
print tup3
```

When the above code is executed, it produces the following result −

```
(12, 34.56, 'abc', 'xyz')
```

Delete Tuple Elements

Removing individual tuple elements is not possible. There is, of course, nothing wrong with putting together another tuple with the undesired elements discarded. To explicitly remove an entire tuple, just use the **del** statement. For example:

```
print tup
del tup;
print "After deleting tup : "
print tup
```

This produces the following result. Note an exception raised, this is because after **del tup** tuple does not exist anymore −

Basic Tuples Operations

Tuples respond to the + and * operators much like strings; they mean concatenation and repetition here too, except that the result is a new tuple, not a string. In fact, tuples respond to all of the general sequence operations we used on strings in the prior chapter −

Python Expression	Results	Description
len((1, 2, 3))	3	Length
(1, 2, 3) + (4, 5, 6)	(1, 2, 3, 4, 5, 6)	Concatenation
('Hi!',) * 4	('Hi!', 'Hi!', 'Hi!', 'Hi!')	Repetition
3 in (1, 2, 3)	True	Membership
for x in (1, 2, 3): print x,	1 2 3	Iteration

Dictionaries

A dictionary is a mapping of key value pairs. The idea comes from our own word dictionary, which consists of words and their meanings. Likewise, a data structures dictionary consists of keys and values that are associated with those keys (like definitions, but less so).

There is one important aspect to a dictionary that you need to understand. The key to a dictionary can be any valid object type. The key, however, must be an immutable value type. That is, you can't use lists as keys in a Python dictionary.

There are a variety of reasons for this, but the major one is that dictionaries are allocated in a fixed way, so that allowing change would overly complicate the underlying code. However, this requirement does explain the need for tuples in Python. The entire purpose of a tuple is to provide an immutable construct. Needless to say, you can use tuples as value types in dictionaries.

Creating a Dictionary

The first step toward working with any new data structure is creating one, and dictionaries are certainly no exception to that rule. As we have seen, Python is all about creating things using strange syntax. The dictionary uses yet another odd character set to define it, in this case the braces ({}) characters:

```
>>> dict = {}
```

This line creates an empty dictionary. There is no particular reason why a new dictionary has to be empty. We could easily create one that had an initial element:

```
>>> dict2 = { "fred":"1010 Elm Street" }
>>> print dict2
{'fred': '1010 Elm Street'}
```

Multiple entries into a dictionary are made by separating them by a comma in the construction phase:

```
>>> dict3 = { "fred":"1010 Elm Street",
"ralph":"2020 Maple Lane" }
>>> print dict3
{'ralph': '2020 Maple Lane', 'fred': '1010 Elm
Street'}
```

The above code creates a dictionary with two keys in it, 'ralph' and 'fred'. Note that the order of things in a dictionary is not guaranteed in any way. We created the dictionary with 'fred' first and 'ralph' second, but when we printed them they were in the opposite order.

Adding to a Dictionary

After you have defined a dictionary, the next logical step is to add new items to it. The syntax for adding items to a dictionary is actually amazingly simple, especially compared to some of the other methods used in Python:

```
>>> dict3['irving'] = '2662 Fremont Blvd'
>>> print dict3
{'ralph': '2020 Maple Lane', 'irving': '2662
Fremont Blvd', 'fred': '1010
Elm Street'}
```

To add a new key value, you simply use the indexing method to define it as a key for the dictionary. Likewise, if you want to change the value for a given entry in a dictionary, you use the same syntax:

```
>>> dict3['fred'] = '1020 Elm Street'
>>> print dict3
{'ralph': '2020 Maple Lane', 'irving': '2662
Fremont Blvd', 'fred': '1020 Elm Street'}
```

You can add or update key values using the same method. This is rather handy, especially if you aren't sure if a given key exists in the dictionary. If you want to know if a dictionary has a given value, you can use the **has_key** method:

Retrieving Values for Keys

When you have added keys and associated values to a dictionary, the real question is how do you get them back? There are a couple of ways to get data back from a key. The first uses the same syntax as setting the data:

```
>>> print dict3['ralph']
2020 Maple Lane
```

There is also a method called get(), which will return either the value of a key, or a default value, depending on whether or not the key was found in the dictionary. The thought process goes like this. If there is a key in the dictionary for the requested key value, return it. If there is no key value, you probably want to do something with it anyway, so allow the programmer to define a default value to return that can be set in the dictionary. You use the get() method this way:

```
>>> dict3.get('ralph', 99)
99
```

Delete Dictionary Elements

You can either remove individual dictionary elements or clear the entire contents of a dictionary. You can also delete entire dictionary in a single operation. To explicitly remove an entire dictionary, just use the **del** statement. Following is a simple example −

```
dict = {'Name': 'abc', 'Age': 7, 'Class': 'First'}

del dict['Name']; # remove entry with key 'Name'
dict.clear();     # remove all entries in dict
del dict ;        # delete entire dictionary

print "dict['Age']: ", dict['Age']
print "dict['School']: ", dict['School']
```

OR

```
>>> del dict['bert']
>>> print dict
```

{'devon': 4, 'adam': 1, 'charlie': 3}

That's all there is to it. Once you've deleted an item from a dictionary, it is gone forever, never to rear its head again. With that, we complete our discussion of dictionaries, and wrap up our discussion of the basic types in Python.

Operators

There are two different kinds of operators in Python, as in most languages. First, there are unary operators. Unary operators are those that operate on a single value. Python supports the basic binary operators that you would expect. Operators are the constructs which can manipulate the value of operands.

Types of Operator

Python language supports the following types of operators.

Arithmetic Operators

Arithmetic Operators

Operator	Description	Example
+ Addition	Adds values on either side of the operator.	a + b = 30
- Subtraction	Subtracts right hand operand from left hand operand.	a − b = -10
* Multiplication	Multiplies values on either side of the operator	a * b = 200
/ Division	Divides left hand operand by right hand operand	b / a = 2
% Modulus	Divides left hand operand by right hand operand and returns remainder	b % a = 0
** Exponent	Performs exponential (power) calculation on operators	a**b =10 to the power 20
//	Floor Division - The division of operands where the result is the quotient in which the digits after the decimal point are removed. But if one of the operands is negative, the result is floored, i.e., rounded away from zero (towards negative infinity):	9//2 = 4 and 9.0//2.0 = 4.0, -11//3 = -4, -11.0//3 = -4.0

Example

```
a = 21
b = 10
c = 0

c = a + b
print "Line 1 - Value of c is ", c

c = a - b
print "Line 2 - Value of c is ", c

c = a * b
print "Line 3 - Value of c is ", c

c = a / b
print "Line 4 - Value of c is ", c

c = a % b
print "Line 5 - Value of c is ", c

a = 2
b = 3
c = a**b
print "Line 6 - Value of c is ", c

a = 10
b = 5
c = a//b
print "Line 7 - Value of c is ", c
```

When you execute the above program, it produces the following result —

```
Line 1 - Value of c is 31
Line 2 - Value of c is 11
Line 3 - Value of c is 210
Line 4 - Value of c is 2
Line 5 - Value of c is 1
Line 6 - Value of c is 8
Line 7 - Value of c is 2
```

Comparison Operators

These operators compare the values on either sides of them and decide the relation among them. They are also called Relational operators.

Operator	Description	Example
==	If the values of two operands are equal, then the condition becomes true.	(a == b) is not true.
!=	If values of two operands are not equal, then condition becomes true.	
>	If the value of left operand is greater than the value of right operand, then condition becomes true.	(a > b) is not true.
<	If the value of left operand is less than the value of right operand, then condition becomes true.	(a < b) is true.
>=	If the value of left operand is greater than or equal to the value of right operand, then condition becomes true.	(a >= b) is not true.
<=	If the value of left operand is less than or equal to the value of right operand, then condition becomes true.	(a <= b) is true.

Example

```
a = 21
b = 10
c = 0

if ( a == b ):
```

```
   print "Line 1 - a is equal to b"
else:
   print "Line 1 - a is not equal to b"

if ( a != b ):
   print "Line 2 - a is not equal to b"
else:
   print "Line 2 - a is equal to b"

if ( a <> b ):
   print "Line 3 - a is not equal to b"
else:
   print "Line 3 - a is equal to b"

if ( a < b ):
   print "Line 4 - a is less than b"
else:
   print "Line 4 - a is not less than b"

if ( a > b ):
   print "Line 5 - a is greater than b"
else:
   print "Line 5 - a is not greater than b"

a = 5;
b = 20;
if ( a <= b ):
   print "Line 6 - a is either less than or equal
to  b"
else:
   print "Line 6 - a is neither less than nor
equal to  b"

if ( b >= a ):
   print "Line 7 - b is either greater than  or
equal to b"
else:
   print "Line 7 - b is neither greater than  nor
equal to b"
```

When you execute the above program it produces the following result −

Line 1 - a is not equal to b
Line 2 - a is not equal to b
Line 3 - a is not equal to b
Line 4 - a is not less than b
Line 5 - a is greater than b
Line 6 - a is either less than or equal to b
Line 7 - b is either greater than or equal to b

Assignment Operators

Operator	Description	Example
=	Assigns values from right side operands to left side operand	c = a + b assigns value of a + b into c
+= Add AND	It adds right operand to the left operand and assign the result to left operand	c += a is equivalent to c = c + a
-= Subtract AND	It subtracts right operand from the left operand and assign the result to left operand	c -= a is equivalent to c = c - a
*= Multiply AND	It multiplies right operand with the left operand and assign the result to left operand	c *= a is equivalent to c = c * a
/= Divide AND	It divides left operand with the right operand and assign the result to left operand	c /= a is equivalent to c = c / ac /= a is equivalent to c = c / a
%= Modulus AND	It takes modulus using two operands and assign the result to left operand	c %= a is equivalent to c = c % a
**= Exponent AND	Performs exponential (power) calculation on operators and assign value to the left operand	c **= a is equivalent to c = c ** a
//= Floor Division	It performs floor division on operators and assign value to the left operand	c //= a is equivalent to c = c // a

Example

Assume variable a holds 10 and variable b holds 20, then −

```
a = 21
b = 10
c = 0

c = a + b
print "Line 1 - Value of c is ", c

c += a
print "Line 2 - Value of c is ", c

c *= a
print "Line 3 - Value of c is ", c

c /= a
print "Line 4 - Value of c is ", c

c  = 2
c %= a
print "Line 5 - Value of c is ", c

c **= a
print "Line 6 - Value of c is ", c

c //= a
print "Line 7 - Value of c is ", c
```

When you execute the above program, it produces the following result −

Line 1 - Value of c is 31
Line 2 - Value of c is 52
Line 3 - Value of c is 1092
Line 4 - Value of c is 52
Line 5 - Value of c is 2
Line 6 - Value of c is 2097152
Line 7 - Value of c is 99864

Logical Operators

The next batch of operators we are going to discuss is the set known as logical operators. These operators are called this because they are used by the logic statement in Python. The set of operators is shown.

Operator name	Purpose
or	Logical or statement
and	Logical and statement
not	Logical not statement

The logical operators are generally used in conditional statements, such as the 'if' statement. For example, consider the following scenario: you want a number that is between 1 and 10, Inclusive. That is, the values 1, 2, 3, 4, 5, 6, 7, 8, 9 and 10 are legitimate, all other values should Be rejected. You could write something like this:

```
if x < 1:
print "Error!"
if x > 10:
print "Error"
# Otherwise, legitimate value.
This, of course, works fine as you would expect:
>>> x = 1
>>> if x < 1:
print "Error"
>>> if x > 10:
print "Error"
>>> x = -1
>>> if x < 1:
print "Error"
Error
>>>
```

Bitwise Operators

The computer world, however, often deals in much smaller increments than True and False. Computer programmers are taught early on to think in terms of bits. A bit is a single 0 or 1 value. In many cases, especially in older applications, a lot of data was stored as individual bits within a numeric value.

Bitwise operator works on bits and performs bit by bit operation. Assume if a = 60; and b = 13; now in binary format they will be as follows –

a = 0011 1100
b = 0000 1101

----

a&b = 0000 1100
a|b = 0011 1101
a^b = 0011 0001
~a = 1100 0011

There are following Bitwise operators supported by Python language

Operator	Description	Example
& Binary AND	Operator copies a bit to the result if it exists in both operands	(a & b) (means 0000 1100)
| Binary OR	It copies a bit if it exists in either operand.	(a | b) = 61 (means 0011 1101)
^ Binary XOR	It copies the bit if it is set in one operand but not both.	(a ^ b) = 49 (means 0011 0001)
~ Binary Ones Complement	It is unary and has the effect of 'flipping' bits.	(~a) = -61 (means 1100 0011 in 2's complement form due to a signed binary number.
<< Binary Left Shift	The left operands value is moved left by the number of bits specified by the right operand.	a << = 240 (means 1111 0000)
>> Binary	The left operands value is	a >> = 15 (means 0000

Right Shift	moved right by the number of bits specified by the right operand.	1111)

Example

```
#!/usr/bin/python

a = 60                  # 60 = 0011 1100
b = 13                  # 13 = 0000 1101
c = 0

c = a & b;              # 12 = 0000 1100
print "Line 1 - Value of c is ", c

c = a | b;              # 61 = 0011 1101
print "Line 2 - Value of c is ", c

c = a ^ b;              # 49 = 0011 0001
print "Line 3 - Value of c is ", c

c = ~a;                 # -61 = 1100 0011
print "Line 4 - Value of c is ", c

c = a << 2;             # 240 = 1111 0000
print "Line 5 - Value of c is ", c

c = a >> 2;             # 15 = 0000 1111
print "Line 6 - Value of c is ", c
```

When you execute the above program it produces the following result –

Line 1 - Value of c is 12
Line 2 - Value of c is 61
Line 3 - Value of c is 49
Line 4 - Value of c is -61
Line 5 - Value of c is 240
Line 6 - Value of c is 15

Decision Making

Decision making is anticipation of conditions occurring while execution of the program and specifying actions taken according to the conditions.

Decision structures evaluate multiple expressions which produce TRUE or FALSE as outcome. You need to determine which action to take and which statements to execute if outcome is TRUE or FALSE otherwise.

Following is the general form of a typical decision making structure found in most of the programming languages −

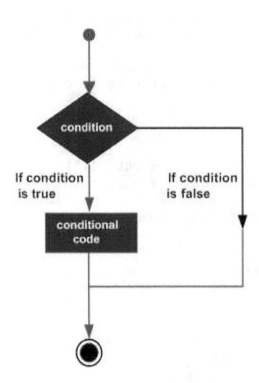

Python programming language assumes any non-zero and non-null values as true, and if it is either zero or null, then it is assumed as false value. Python programming language provides following types of decision making statements.

Statement	Description
if statements	An **if statement** consists of a Boolean expression followed by one or more statements.
if...else statements	An **if statement** can be followed by an optional **else statement**, which executes when the Boolean expression is FALSE.
nested if statements	You can use one **if** or **else if** statement inside another **if** or **else if** statement(s).

IF Statement

It is similar to that of other languages. The **if** statement contains a logical expression using which data is compared and a decision is made based on the result of the comparison.

Syntax

```
if expression:
   statement(s)
```

If the boolean expression evaluates to true, then the block of statement(s) inside the if statement is executed. If boolean expression evaluates to false, then the first set of code after the end of the if statement(s) is executed.

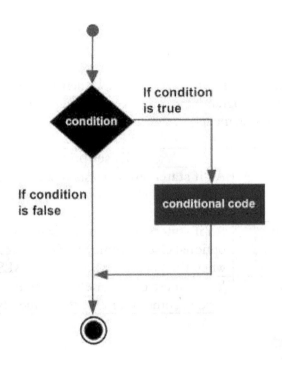

Example

```
var1 = 100
if var1:
    print "1 - Got a true expression value"
    print var1
var2 = 0
if var2:
    print "2 - Got a true expression value"
    print var2
print "Good bye!"
```

When the above code is executed, it produces the following result −

```
1 - Got a true expression value
100
Good bye!
```

IF...ELIF...ELSE Statements

An else statement can be combined with an if statement. An else statement contains the block of code that executes if the conditional expression in the if statement resolves to 0 or a FALSE value. The *else* statement is an optional statement and there could be at most only one else statement following if .

Syntax

```
if expression:
    statement(s)
else:
    statement(s)
```

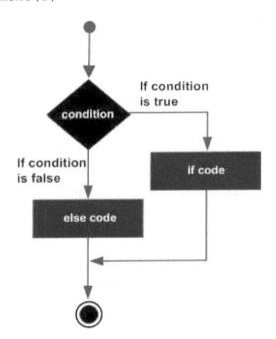

Example

```
var1 = 100
if var1:
```

```
    print "1 - Got a true expression value"
    print var1
else:
    print "1 - Got a false expression value"
    print var1

var2 = 0
if var2:
    print "2 - Got a true expression value"
    print var2
else:
    print "2 - Got a false expression value"
    print var2

print "Good bye!"
```

When the above code is executed, it produces the following result —
```
1 - Got a true expression value
100
2 - Got a false expression value
0
Good bye!
```

The elif Statement

The **elif** statement allows you to check multiple expressions for TRUE and execute a block of code as soon as one of the conditions evaluates to TRUE.

Similar to the **else**, the **elif** statement is optional. However, unlike **else**, for which there can be at most one statement, there can be an arbitrary number of **elif** statements following an **if**.

syntax

```
if expression1:
    statement(s)
elif expression2:
    statement(s)
```

```
elif expression3:
    statement(s)
else:
    statement(s)
```

Core python does not provide switch or case statements as in other languages, but we can use if..elif...statements to simulate switch case as follows −

Example

```
var = 100
if var == 200:
    print "1 - Got a true expression value"
    print var
elif var == 150:
    print "2 - Got a true expression value"
    print var
elif var == 100:
    print "3 - Got a true expression value"
    print var
else:
    print "4 - Got a false expression value"
    print var

print "Good bye!"
```

When the above code is executed, it produces the following result −

```
3 - Got a true expression value
100
Good bye!
```

nested IF statements

There may be a situation when you want to check for another condition after a condition resolves to true. In such a situation, you can use the nested **if** construct.In a nested **if** construct, you can have an **if...elif...else** construct inside another **if...elif...else** construct.

Syntax:

```
if expression1:
   statement(s)
   if expression2:
      statement(s)
   elif expression3:
      statement(s)
   else:
      statement(s)
elif expression4:
   statement(s)
else:
   statement(s)
```

Example:

```
var = 100
if var < 200:
   print "Expression value is less than 200"
   if var == 150:
      print "Which is 150"
   elif var == 100:
      print "Which is 100"
   elif var == 50:
      print "Which is 50"
elif var < 50:
   print "Expression value is less than 50"
else:
   print "Could not find true expression"

print "Good bye!"
```

When the above code is executed, it produces following result:

```
Expression value is less than 200
Which is 100
Good bye!
```

Loops

Modern programming languages all contain some sort of looping mechanism. Some contain Quite a few different varieties, from for loops, to do loops, to while loops, to repeat Until loops. Python contains two varieties of looping constructs. First, there is the for loop, Which is the main workhorse for looping.

The for loop in Python can do pretty much anything Any other sort of loop can do, and then some. If that were not enough, Python contains the While loop, which is more of a conditional looping structure than anything else. In this section, we will take a look at the two kinds of loops and how they work in Python.

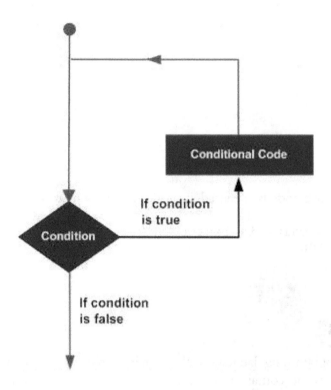

while Loop Statements

A while loop statement in Python programming language repeatedly executes a target statement as long as a given condition is true.

Syntax

The syntax of a **while** loop in Python programming language is −

```
while expression:
    statement(s)
```

Here, **statement(s)** may be a single statement or a block of statements. The **condition** may be any expression, and true is any non-zero value. The loop iterates while the condition is true. When the condition becomes false, program control passes to the line immediately following the loop.

In Python, all the statements indented by the same number of character spaces after a programming construct are considered to be part of a single block of code. Python uses indentation as its method of grouping statements.

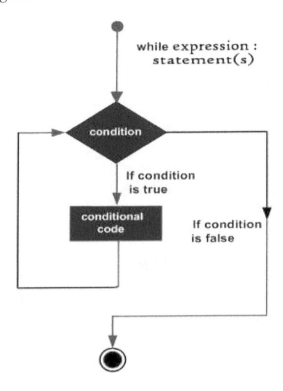

Here, key point of the while loop is that the loop might not ever run. When the condition is tested and the result is false, the loop body will be skipped and the first statement after the while loop will be executed.

Example

```
count = 0
while (count < 9):
    print 'The count is:', count
    count = count + 1

print "Good bye!"
```

When the above code is executed, it produces the following result −

```
The count is: 0
The count is: 1
The count is: 2
The count is: 3
The count is: 4
The count is: 5
The count is: 6
The count is: 7
The count is: 8
Good bye!
```

for Loop Statements

The for loop is the basic looping structure in python. It has the ability to iterate over the items of any sequence, such as a list or a string.

Syntax

```
for iterating_var in sequence:
    statements(s)
```

If a sequence contains an expression list, it is evaluated first. Then, the first item in the sequence is assigned to the iterating variable *iterating_var*. Next, the statements block is executed. Each item in the list is assigned to *iterating_var*, and the statement(s) block is executed until the entire sequence is exhausted.

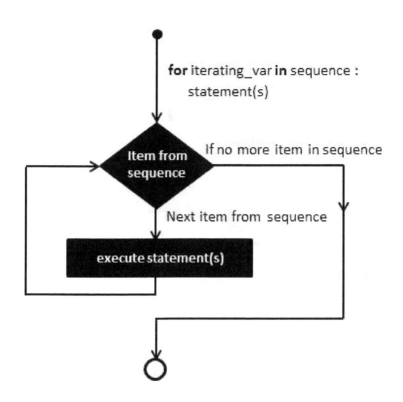

Example

```
for letter in 'Python':       # First Example
   print 'Current Letter :', letter

fruits = ['banana', 'apple',  'mango']
for fruit in fruits:          # Second Example
   print 'Current fruit :', fruit

print "Good bye!"
```

When the above code is executed, it produces the following result −

```
Current Letter : P
Current Letter : y
Current Letter : t
Current Letter : h
Current Letter : o
```

```
Current Letter : n
Current fruit : banana
Current fruit : apple
Current fruit : mango
Good bye!
```

Iterating by Sequence Index

An alternative way of iterating through each item is by index offset into the sequence itself. Following is a simple example −

```
fruits = ['banana', 'apple',  'mango']
for index in range(len(fruits)):
   print 'Current fruit :', fruits[index]

print "Good bye!"
```

When the above code is executed, it produces the following result −

```
Current fruit : banana
Current fruit : apple
Current fruit : mango
Good bye!
```

nested loops

Python programming language allows to use one loop inside another loop. Following section shows few examples to illustrate the concept.

Syntax

```
for iterating_var in sequence:
   for iterating_var in sequence:
      statements(s)
   statements(s)
```

The syntax for a **nested while loop** statement in python programming language is as follows −

```
while expression:
    while expression:
        statement(s)
    statement(s)
```

A final note on loop nesting is that you can put any type of loop inside of any other type of loop. For example a for loop can be inside a while loop or vice versa.

Example

The following program uses a nested for loop to find the prime numbers from 2 to 100 −

```
i = 2
while(i < 100):
    j = 2
    while(j <= (i/j)):
        if not(i%j): break
        j = j + 1
    if (j > i/j) : print i, " is prime"
    i = i + 1

print "Good bye!"
```

Python Input & Output

Without user input, the computer world would surely be extremely boring to the end user. In order to have any sort of control over what comes out of the system, you have to have some control over what goes into the system. That system input is usually in the form of the user being prompted for information and entering the requested information into the system in the easiest and most straightforward method possible. The two most basic functions provided with the Python environment are **input()** and **raw_input()**.

Printing to the Screen

The simplest way to produce output is using the *print* statement where you can pass zero or more expressions separated by commas. This function converts the expressions you pass into a string and writes the result to standard output as follows –

```
print "Python is really a great language,",
"isn't it?"
```

This produces the following result on your standard screen –

```
Python is really a great language, isn't it?
```

Reading Keyboard Input

Python provides two built-in functions to read a line of text from standard input, which by default comes from the keyboard. These functions are – input() **and** raw_input().

The raw_input Function

The raw_input([prompt]) function reads one line from standard input and returns it as a string (removing the trailing newline).

```
str = raw_input("Enter your input: ");
print "Received input is : ", str
```

This prompts you to enter any string and it would display same string on the screen. When I typed "Hello Python!", its output is like this –

```
Enter your input: Hello Python
Received input is :  Hello Python
```

The input Function

The input([prompt]) function is equivalent to raw_input, except that it assumes the input is a valid Python expression and returns the evaluated result to you.

```
str = input("Enter your input: ");
print "Received input is : ", str
```

This would produce the following result against the entered input –

```
Enter your input: [x*5 for x in range(2,10,2)]
Received input is :   [10, 20, 30, 40]
```

Opening and Closing Files

Until now, you have been reading and writing to the standard input and output. Now, we will see how to use actual data files. Python provides basic functions and methods necessary to manipulate files by default. You can do most of the file manipulation using a **file** object.

The open Function

Before you can read or write a file, you have to open it using Python's built-in open() function. This function creates a file object, which would be utilized to call other support methods associated with it.

Syntax

```
file object = open(file_name [, access_mode] [,
buffering])
```

Example

```
# Open a file
fo = open("foo.txt", "wb")
print "Name of the file: ", fo.name
print "Closed or not : ", fo.closed
print "Opening mode : ", fo.mode
print "Softspace flag : ", fo.softspace
```

This produces the following result –

```
Name of the file:  foo.txt
Closed or not :  False
Opening mode :  wb
Softspace flag :  0
```

The close() Method

The close() method of a *file* object flushes any unwritten information and closes the file object, after which no more writing can be done.

Python automatically closes a file when the reference object of a file is reassigned to another file. It is a good practice to use the close() method to close a file.

Syntax

```
fileObject.close();
```

Example

```
# Open a file
fo = open("foo.txt", "wb")
print "Name of the file: ", fo.name

# Close opend file
fo.close()
```

This produces the following result −

```
Name of the file:  foo.txt
```

Reading and Writing Files

The file object provides a set of access methods to make our lives easier. We would see how to use read() and write() methods to read and write files.

The write() Method

The *write()* method writes any string to an open file. It is important to note that Python strings can have binary data and not just text.The write() method does not add a newline character ('\n') to the end of the string −

Syntax

```
fileObject.write(string);
```

Example

```
# Open a file
fo = open("foo.txt", "wb")
fo.write( "Python is a great language.\nYeah its
great!!\n");

# Close opend file
fo.close()
```

The above method would create *foo.txt* file and would write given content in that file and finally it would close that file. If you would open this file, it would have following content.

```
Python is a great language.
Yeah its great!!
```

The read() Method

The *read()* method reads a string from an open file. It is important to note that Python strings can have binary data. apart from text data.

Syntax

```
fileObject.read([count]);
```

Here, passed parameter is the number of bytes to be read from the opened file. This method starts reading from the beginning of the file and if *count* is missing, then it tries to read as much as possible, maybe until the end of file.

Example

```
# Open a file
fo = open("foo.txt", "r+")
str = fo.read(10);
```

```
print "Read String is : ", str
# Close opend file
fo.close()
```

This produces the following result −

```
Read String is :  Python is
```

Functions

The single biggest difference between early, first generation programming languages and later programming languages is the addition of functions. Functions made it possible to stop copying blocks of code from one place to another and to begin the process of reusing code entities. A function is a block of organized, reusable code that is used to perform a single, related action. Functions provide better modularity for your application and a high degree of code reusing.

As you already know, Python gives you many built-in functions like print(), etc. but you can also create your own functions. These functions are called *user-defined functions.*

Defining a Function

You can define functions to provide the required functionality. Here are simple rules to define a function in Python.

Function blocks begin with the keyword **def** followed by the function name and parentheses (( )).

Any input parameters or arguments should be placed within these parentheses. You can also define parameters inside these parentheses.

The first statement of a function can be an optional statement - the documentation string of the function or *docstring.*

The code block within every function starts with a colon (:) and is indented.

The statement return [expression] exits a function, optionally passing back an expression to the caller. A return statement with no arguments is the same as return None.

Syntax

```
def functionname( parameters ):
    "function_docstring"
    function_suite
    return [expression]
```

By default, parameters have a positional behavior and you need to inform them in the same order that they were defined.

Example

The following function takes a string as input parameter and prints it on standard screen.

```
def printme( str ):
  "This prints a passed string into this function"
    print str
    return
```

Calling a Function

Defining a function only gives it a name, specifies the parameters that are to be included in the function and structures the blocks of code.

Once the basic structure of a function is finalized, you can execute it by calling it from another function or directly from the Python prompt. Following is the example to call printme() function –

```
# Function definition is here
def printme( str ):
    "This prints a passed string into this
function"
```

```
    print str
    return;

# Now you can call printme function
printme("I'm first call to user defined
function!")
printme("Again second call to the same function")
```

Function Arguments

You can call a function by using the following types of formal arguments:

- Required arguments
- Keyword arguments
- Default arguments
- Variable-length arguments

Required arguments

Required arguments are the arguments passed to a function in correct positional order. Here, the number of arguments in the function call should match exactly with the function definition.To call the function *printme()*, you definitely need to pass one argument, otherwise it gives a syntax error as follows –

```
# Function definition is here
def printme( str ):
    "This prints a passed string into this
function"
    print str
    return;

# Now you can call printme function
printme()
```

When the above code is executed, it produces the following result:

```
Traceback (most recent call last):
  File "test.py", line 11, in <module>
    printme();
```

```
TypeError: printme() takes exactly 1 argument (0
given)
```

Keyword arguments

Keyword arguments are related to the function calls. When you use keyword arguments in a function call, the caller identifies the arguments by the parameter name.

This allows you to skip arguments or place them out of order because the Python interpreter is able to use the keywords provided to match the values with parameters. You can also make keyword calls to the *printme()* function in the following ways –

```
# Function definition is here
def printme( str ):
    "This prints a passed string into this
function"
    print str
    return;

# Now you can call printme function
printme( str = "My string")
```

When the above code is executed, it produces the following result –

```
My string
```

The following example gives more clear picture. Note that the order of parameters does not matter.

```
# Function definition is here
def printinfo( name, age ):
    "This prints a passed info into this function"
    print "Name: ", name
    print "Age ", age
    return;

# Now you can call printinfo function
printinfo( age=50, name="miki" )
```

When the above code is executed, it produces the following result –

```
Name:  miki
Age   50
```

Default arguments

A default argument is an argument that assumes a default value if a value is not provided in the function call for that argument. The following example gives an idea on default arguments, it prints default age if it is not passed −

```
# Function definition is here
def printinfo( name, age = 35 ):
   "This prints a passed info into this function"
   print "Name: ", name
   print "Age ", age
   return;

# Now you can call printinfo function
printinfo( age=50, name="miki" )
printinfo( name="miki" )
```

When the above code is executed, it produces the following result −

```
Name:  miki
Age   50
Name:  miki
Age   35
```

Python Modules

A module allows you to logically organize your Python code. Grouping related code into a module makes the code easier to understand and use. A module is a Python object with arbitrarily named attributes that you can bind and reference.

Simply, a module is a file consisting of Python code. A module can define functions, classes and variables. A module can also include runnable code.

Example

The Python code for a module named *aname* normally resides in a file named *aname.py*. Here's an example of a simple module, support.py

```
def print_func( par ):
   print "Hello : ", par
   return
```

The import Statement

You can use any Python source file as a module by executing an import statement in some other Python source file. The *import* has the following syntax:

```
import module1[, module2[,... moduleN]
```

When the interpreter encounters an import statement, it imports the module if the module is present in the search path. A search path is a list of directories that the interpreter searches before importing a module. For example, to import the module support.py, you need to put the following command at the top of the script −

```
# Import module support
import support

# Now you can call defined function that module
as follows
support.print_func("mypyhton")
```

When the above code is executed, it produces the following result −

```
Hello : mypython
```

A module is loaded only once, regardless of the number of times it is imported. This prevents the module execution from happening over and over again if multiple imports occur.

The from...import Statement

Python's *from* statement lets you import specific attributes from a module into the current namespace. The *from...import* has the following syntax −

```
from modname import name1[, name2[, ... nameN]]
```

For example, to import the function Fibonacci from the module fib, use the following statement −

```
from fib import Fibonacci
```

This statement does not import the entire module fib into the current namespace; it just introduces the item Fibonacci from the module fib into the global symbol table of the importing module.

The from...import * Statement:

It is also possible to import all names from a module into the current namespace by using the following import statement −

```
from modname import *
```

This provides an easy way to import all the items from a module into the current namespace; however, this statement should be used sparingly.

Locating Modules

When you import a module, the Python interpreter searches for the module in the following sequences −

- The current directory.

- If the module isn't found, Python then searches each directory in the shell variable PYTHONPATH.
- If all else fails, Python checks the default path. On UNIX, this default path is normally /usr/local/lib/python/.

The module search path is stored in the system module sys as the **sys.path** variable. The sys.path variable contains the current directory, PYTHONPATH, and the installation-dependent default.

The PYTHONPATH Variable:

The PYTHONPATH is an environment variable, consisting of a list of directories. The syntax of PYTHONPATH is the same as that of the shell variable PATH.

Here is a typical PYTHONPATH from a Windows system:

```
set PYTHONPATH=c:\python3\lib;
```

And here is a typical pythonpath from a unix system:

```
set PYTHONPATH=/usr/local/lib/python
```

Namespaces and Scoping

Variables are names (identifiers) that map to objects. A *namespace* is a dictionary of variable names (keys) and their corresponding objects (values).

A Python statement can access variables in a *local namespace* and in the *global namespace*. If a local and a global variable have the same name, the local variable shadows the global variable.

Each function has its own local namespace. Class methods follow the same scoping rule as ordinary functions.

Python makes educated guesses on whether variables are local or global. It assumes that any variable assigned a value in a function is local.

Therefore, in order to assign a value to a global variable within a function, you must first use the global statement.

The statement *global VarName* tells Python that VarName is a global variable. Python stops searching the local namespace for the variable.

For example, we define a variable *Money* in the global namespace. Within the function *Money*, we assign *Money* a value, therefore Python assumes *Money* as a local variable. However, we accessed the value of the local variable *Money* before setting it, so an UnboundLocalError is the result. Uncommenting the global statement fixes the problem.

```
Money = 2000
def AddMoney():
    # Uncomment the following line to fix the
code:
    # global Money
    Money = Money + 1

print Money
AddMoney()
print Money
```

The dir( ) Function

The dir() built-in function returns a sorted list of strings containing the names defined by a module.

The list contains the names of all the modules, variables and functions that are defined in a module. Following is a simple example

```
import math
content = dir(math)
print content
```

When the above code is executed, it produces the following result −

```
['__doc__', '__file__', '__name__', 'acos',
'asin', 'atan',
'atan2', 'ceil', 'cos', 'cosh', 'degrees', 'e',
'exp',
'fabs', 'floor', 'fmod', 'frexp', 'hypot',
'ldexp', 'log',
'log10', 'modf', 'pi', 'pow', 'radians', 'sin',
'sinh',
'sqrt', 'tan', 'tanh']
```

Here, the special string variable __*name*__ is the module's name, and __*file*__ is the filename from which the module was loaded.

The globals() and locals() Functions −

The *globals()* and *locals()* functions can be used to return the names in the global and local namespaces depending on the location from where they are called.

If locals() is called from within a function, it will return all the names that can be accessed locally from that function.

If globals() is called from within a function, it will return all the names that can be accessed globally from that function.

The return type of both these functions is dictionary. Therefore, names can be extracted using the keys() function.

The reload() Function

When the module is imported into a script, the code in the top-level portion of a module is executed only once.

Therefore, if you want to reexecute the top-level code in a module, you can use the *reload()* function. The reload() function imports a previously imported module again. The syntax of the reload() function is this −

```
reload(module_name)
```

Here, *module_name* is the name of the module you want to reload and not the string containing the module name. For example, to reload *hello* module, do the following −

```
reload(hello)
```

Packages in Python

A package is a hierarchical file directory structure that defines a single Python application environment that consists of modules and subpackages and sub-subpackages, and so on.

Consider a file *Pots.py* available in *Phone* directory. This file has following line of source code −

```
def Pots():
    print "I'm Pots Phone"
```

Similar way, we have another two files having different functions with the same name as above −

- *Phone/Isdn.py* file having function Isdn()
- *Phone/G3.py* file having function G3()

Now, create one more file __init__.py in *phone* directory −

Phone/__init__.py

To make all of your functions available when you've imported phone, you need to put explicit import statements in __init__.py as follows −

```
from Pots import Pots
from Isdn import Isdn
from G3 import G3
```

After you add these lines to __init__.py, you have all of these classes available when you import the Phone package.

```
# Now import your Phone Package.
import Phone

Phone.Pots()
Phone.Isdn()
Phone.G3()
```

When the above code is executed, it produces the following result −

```
I'm Pots Phone
I'm 3G Phone
I'm ISDN Phone
```

In the above example, we have taken example of a single functions in each file, but you can keep multiple functions in your files. You can also define different Python classes in those files and then you can create your packages out of those classes.

Python Exceptions Handling

What is Exception?

An exception is an event, which occurs during the execution of a program that disrupts the normal flow of the program's instructions. In general, when a Python script encounters a situation that it cannot cope with, it raises an exception. An exception is a Python object that represents an error.

When a Python script raises an exception, it must either handle the exception immediately otherwise it terminates and quits.

Handling an exception

If you have some *suspicious* code that may raise an exception, you can defend your program by placing the suspicious code in a try: block. After the try: block, include an except: statement, followed by a block of code which handles the problem as elegantly as possible.

Syntax

Here is simple syntax of *try....except...else* blocks —

```
try:
   You do your operations here;
   .....................
except ExceptionI:
   If there is ExceptionI, then execute this
block.
except ExceptionII:
   If there is ExceptionII, then execute this
block.
   .....................
else:
   If there is no exception then execute this
block.
```

Here are few important points about the above-mentioned syntax —

1. A single try statement can have multiple except statements. This is useful when the try block contains statements that may throw different types of exceptions.
2. You can also provide a generic except clause, which handles any exception.
3. After the except clause(s), you can include an else-clause. The code in the else-block executes if the code in the try: block does not raise an exception.
4. The else-block is a good place for code that does not need the try: block's protection.

Example

This example opens a file, writes content in the, file and comes out gracefully because there is no problem at all —

```
try:
    fh = open("testfile", "w")
    fh.write("This is my test file for exception
handling!!")
except IOError:
    print "Error: can\'t find file or read data"
else:
    print "Written content in the file
successfully"
    fh.close()
```

This produces the following result —

```
Written content in the file successfully
```

Example

This example tries to open a file where you do not have write permission, so it raises an exception —

```
try:
    fh = open("testfile", "r")
    fh.write("This is my test file for exception
handling!!")
except IOError:
    print "Error: can\'t find file or read data"
else:
    print "Written content in the file
successfully"
```

This produces the following result —

```
Error: can't find file or read data
```

The except Clause with No Exceptions

You can also use the except statement with no exceptions defined as follows −

```
try:
   You do your operations here;
   .....................
except:
   If there is any exception, then execute this
block.
   .....................
else:
   If there is no exception then execute this
block.
```

This kind of a try-except statement catches all the exceptions that occur. Using this kind of try-except statement is not considered a good programming practice though, because it catches all exceptions but does not make the programmer identify the root cause of the problem that may occur.

The *except* Clause with Multiple Exceptions

You can also use the same *except* statement to handle multiple exceptions as follows −

```
try:
   You do your operations here;
   .....................
except(Exception1[,
Exception2[,...ExceptionN]]):
   If there is any exception from the given
exception list,
      then execute this block.
   .....................
else:
   If there is no exception then execute this
block.
```

The try-finally Clause

You can use a finally: block along with a try: block. The finally block is a place to put any code that must execute, whether the try-block raised an exception or not. The syntax of the try-finally statement is this −

```
try:
    You do your operations here;
    ......................
    Due to any exception, this may be skipped.
finally:
    This would always be executed.
    ......................
```

You cannot use *else* clause as well along with a finally clause.

Example

```
try:
    fh = open("testfile", "w")
    fh.write("This is my test file for exception
handling!!")
finally:
    print "Error: can\'t find file or read data"
```

If you do not have permission to open the file in writing mode, then this will produce the following result:

```
Error: can't find file or read data
```

Same example can be written more cleanly as follows −

```
try:
    fh = open("testfile", "w")
    try:
        fh.write("This is my test file for
exception handling!!")
    finally:
        print "Going to close the file"
        fh.close()
```

```
except IOError:
    print "Error: can\'t find file or read data"
```

When an exception is thrown in the *try* block, the execution immediately passes to the *finally* block. After all the statements in the *finally* block are executed, the exception is raised again and is handled in the *except* statements if present in the next higher layer of the *try-except* statement.

Argument of an Exception

An exception can have an *argument*, which is a value that gives additional information about the problem. The contents of the argument vary by exception. You capture an exception's argument by supplying a variable in the except clause as follows −

```
try:
    You do your operations here;
    ......................
except ExceptionType, Argument:
    You can print value of Argument here...
```

If you write the code to handle a single exception, you can have a variable follow the name of the exception in the except statement. If you are trapping multiple exceptions, you can have a variable follow the tuple of the exception.

This variable receives the value of the exception mostly containing the cause of the exception. The variable can receive a single value or multiple values in the form of a tuple. This tuple usually contains the error string, the error number, and an error location.

Example

Following is an example for a single exception −

```
# Define a function here.
def temp_convert(var):
    try:
        return int(var)
```

```
    except ValueError, Argument:
        print "The argument does not contain
numbers\n", Argument

# Call above function here.
temp_convert("xyz");
```

This produces the following result −

```
The argument does not contain numbers
invalid literal for int() with base 10: 'xyz'
```

Raising an Exceptions

You can raise exceptions in several ways by using the raise statement. The general syntax for the raise statement is as follows.

Syntax

```
raise [Exception [, args [, traceback]]]
```

Here, *Exception* is the type of exception (for example, NameError) and *argument* is a value for the exception argument. The argument is optional; if not supplied, the exception argument is None.

The final argument, traceback, is also optional (and rarely used in practice), and if present, is the traceback object used for the exception.

Example

An exception can be a string, a class or an object. Most of the exceptions that the Python core raises are classes, with an argument that is an instance of the class. Defining new exceptions is quite easy and can be done as follows −

```
def functionName( level ):
    if level < 1:
```

```
    raise "Invalid level!", level
    # The code below to this would not be
executed
    # if we raise the exception
```

Note: In order to catch an exception, an "except" clause must refer to the same exception thrown either class object or simple string. For example, to capture above exception, we must write the except clause as follows –

```
try:
    Business Logic here...
except "Invalid level!":
    Exception handling here...
else:
    Rest of the code here...
```

Python provides two very important features to handle any unexpected error in your Python programs and to add debugging capabilities in them –

Exception Handling: Here is a list standard Exceptions available in Python:

EXCEPTION NAME	DESCRIPTION
Exception	Base class for all exceptions
StopIteration	Raised when the next() method of an iterator does not point to any object.
SystemExit	Raised by the sys.exit() function.
StandardError	Base class for all built-in exceptions except StopIteration and SystemExit.
ArithmeticError	Base class for all errors that occur for numeric calculation.
OverflowError	Raised when a calculation exceeds maximum limit for a numeric type.
FloatingPointError	Raised when a floating point calculation fails.
ZeroDivisionError	Raised when division or modulo by zero takes place for all numeric types.

AssertionError	Raised in case of failure of the Assert statement.
AttributeError	Raised in case of failure of attribute reference or assignment.
EOFError	Raised when there is no input from either the raw_input() or input() function and the end of file is reached.
ImportError	Raised when an import statement fails.
KeyboardInterrupt	Raised when the user interrupts program execution, usually by pressing Ctrl+c.
LookupError	Base class for all lookup errors.
IndexError	Raised when an index is not found in a sequence.
KeyError	Raised when the specified key is not found in the dictionary.
NameError	Raised when an identifier is not found in the local or global namespace.
UnboundLocalError	Raised when trying to access a local variable in a function or method but no value has been assigned to it.
EnvironmentError	Base class for all exceptions that occur outside the Python environment.
IOError	Raised when an input/ output operation fails, such as the print statement or the open() function when trying to open a file that does not exist.
OSError	Raised for operating system-related errors.
SyntaxError	Raised when there is an error in Python syntax.
IndentationError	Raised when indentation is not specified properly.
SystemError	Raised when the interpreter finds an internal problem, but when this error is encountered the Python interpreter does not exit.
SystemExit	Raised when Python interpreter is quit by using the sys.exit() function. If not handled in the code, causes the interpreter to exit.
TypeError	Raised when an operation or function is

	attempted that is invalid for the specified data type.
ValueError	Raised when the built-in function for a data type has the valid type of arguments, but the arguments have invalid values specified.
RuntimeError	Raised when a generated error does not fall into any category.
NotImplementedError	Raised when an abstract method that needs to be implemented in an inherited class is not actually implemented.

Assertions in Python

An assertion is a sanity-check that you can turn on or turn off when you are done with your testing of the program.

The easiest way to think of an assertion is to liken it to a **raise-if** statement (or to be more accurate, a raise-if-not statement). An expression is tested, and if the result comes up false, an exception is raised.

Assertions are carried out by the assert statement, the newest keyword to Python, introduced in version 1.5.

Programmers often place assertions at the start of a function to check for valid input, and after a function call to check for valid output.

The assert Statement

When it encounters an assert statement, Python evaluates the accompanying expression, which is hopefully true. If the expression is false, Python raises an *AssertionError* exception.

The syntax for assert is −

```
assert Expression[, Arguments]
```

If the assertion fails, Python uses ArgumentExpression as the argument for the AssertionError. AssertionError exceptions can be caught and handled like any other exception using the try-except statement, but if not handled, they will terminate the program and produce a traceback.

Example

Here is a function that converts a temperature from degrees Kelvin to degrees Fahrenheit. Since zero degrees Kelvin is as cold as it gets, the function bails out if it sees a negative temperature −

```
def KelvinToFahrenheit(Temperature):
    assert (Temperature >= 0),"Colder than
absolute zero!"
    return ((Temperature-273)*1.8)+32
print KelvinToFahrenheit(273)
print int(KelvinToFahrenheit(505.78))
print KelvinToFahrenheit(-5)
```

When the above code is executed, it produces the following result −

```
32.0
451
Traceback (most recent call last):
File "test.py", line 9, in
print KelvinToFahrenheit(-5)
File "test.py", line 4, in KelvinToFahrenheit
assert (Temperature >= 0),"Colder than absolute
zero!"
AssertionError: Colder than absolute zero!
```

Python MySQL Database Access

The Python standard for database interfaces is the Python DB-API. Most Python database interfaces adhere to this standard.

You can choose the right database for your application. Python Database API supports a wide range of database servers such as —

- GadFly
- mSQL
- MySQL
- PostgreSQL
- Microsoft SQL Server 2000
- Informix
- Interbase
- Oracle
- Sybase

Here is the list of available Python database interfaces: Python Database Interfaces and APIs .You must download a separate DB API module for each database you need to access. For example, if you need to access an Oracle database as well as a MySQL database, you must download both the Oracle and the MySQL database modules.

The DB API provides a minimal standard for working with databases using Python structures and syntax wherever possible. This API includes the following:

- Importing the API module.
- Acquiring a connection with the database.
- Issuing SQL statements and stored procedures.
- Closing the connection

We would learn all the concepts using MySQL, so let us talk about MySQLdb module.

What is MySQLdb?

MySQLdb is an interface for connecting to a MySQL database server from Python. It implements the Python Database API v2.0 and is built on top of the MySQL C API.

How do I Install MySQLdb?

Before proceeding, you make sure you have MySQLdb installed on your machine. Just type the following in your Python script and execute it:

```
import MySQLdb
```

If it produces the following result, then it means MySQLdb module is not installed:

```
Traceback (most recent call last):
  File "test.py", line 3, in <module>
    import MySQLdb
ImportError: No module named MySQLdb
```

To install MySQLdb module, use the following command:

```
For Ubuntu, use the following command -
$ sudo apt-get install python-pip python-dev
libmysqlclient-dev
For Fedora, use the following command -
$ sudo dnf install python python-devel mysql-
devel redhat-rpm-config gcc
For Python command prompt, use the following
command -
pip install MySQL-python
```

Note: Make sure you have root privilege to install above module.

Database Connection

Before connecting to a MySQL database, make sure of the followings –

- You have created a database TESTDB.
- You have created a table EMPLOYEE in TESTDB.
- This table has fields FIRST_NAME, LAST_NAME, AGE, SEX and INCOME.

- User ID "testuser" and password "test123" are set to access TESTDB.
- Python module MySQLdb is installed properly on your machine.

Example

Following is the example of connecting with MySQL database "TESTDB"

```
import MySQLdb

# Open database connection
db =
MySQLdb.connect("localhost","testuser","test123",
"TESTDB" )

# prepare a cursor object using cursor() method
cursor = db.cursor()

# execute SQL query using execute() method.
cursor.execute("SELECT VERSION()")

# Fetch a single row using fetchone() method.
data = cursor.fetchone()

print "Database version : %s " % data

# disconnect from server
db.close()
```

While running this script, it is producing the following result in my Linux machine.

```
Database version : 5.0.45
```

If a connection is established with the datasource, then a Connection Object is returned and saved into db for further use, otherwise db is set to None. Next, db object is used to create a cursor object, which in turn is used to execute SQL queries. Finally, before coming out, it ensures that database connection is closed and resources are released.

Creating Database Table

Once a database connection is established, we are ready to create tables or records into the database tables using execute method of the created cursor.

Example

Let us create Database table EMPLOYEE:

```
import MySQLdb

# Open database connection
db =
MySQLdb.connect("localhost","testuser","test123",
"TESTDB" )

# prepare a cursor object using cursor() method
cursor = db.cursor()

# Drop table if it already exist using execute()
method.
cursor.execute("DROP TABLE IF EXISTS EMPLOYEE")

# Create table as per requirement
sql = """CREATE TABLE EMPLOYEE (
         FIRST_NAME  CHAR(20) NOT NULL,
         LAST_NAME   CHAR(20),
         AGE INT,
         SEX CHAR(1),
         INCOME FLOAT ) """

cursor.execute(sql)

# disconnect from server
db.close()
```

INSERT Operation

It is required when you want to create your records into a database table.

Example

The following example, executes SQL *INSERT* statement to create a record into EMPLOYEE table −

```
import MySQLdb

# Open database connection
db =
MySQLdb.connect("localhost","testuser","test123",
"TESTDB" )

# prepare a cursor object using cursor() method
cursor = db.cursor()

# Prepare SQL query to INSERT a record into the
database.
sql = """INSERT INTO EMPLOYEE(FIRST_NAME,
         LAST_NAME, AGE, SEX, INCOME)
         VALUES ('Mac', 'Mohan', 20, 'M',
2000)"""
try:
    # Execute the SQL command
    cursor.execute(sql)
    # Commit your changes in the database
    db.commit()
except:
    # Rollback in case there is any error
    db.rollback()

# disconnect from server
db.close()
```

Above example can be written as follows to create SQL queries dynamically −

```python
import MySQLdb

# Open database connection
db =
MySQLdb.connect("localhost","testuser","test123",
"TESTDB" )

# prepare a cursor object using cursor() method
cursor = db.cursor()

# Prepare SQL query to INSERT a record into the
database.
sql = "INSERT INTO EMPLOYEE(FIRST_NAME, \
       LAST_NAME, AGE, SEX, INCOME) \
       VALUES ('%s', '%s', '%d', '%c', '%d' )" % \
       ('Mac', 'Mohan', 20, 'M', 2000)
try:
   # Execute the SQL command
   cursor.execute(sql)
   # Commit your changes in the database
   db.commit()
except:
   # Rollback in case there is any error
   db.rollback()

# disconnect from server
db.close()
```

Example

Following code segment is another form of execution where you can pass parameters directly —

```python
user_id = "test123"
password = "password"

con.execute('insert into Login values("%s",
"%s")' % \
```

```
(user_id, password))
```

READ Operation

READ Operation on any database means to fetch some useful information from the database.

Once our database connection is established, you are ready to make a query into this database. You can use either **fetchone()** method to fetch single record or **fetchall()** method to fetech multiple values from a database table.

- **fetchone():** It fetches the next row of a query result set. A result set is an object that is returned when a cursor object is used to query a table.
- **fetchall():** It fetches all the rows in a result set. If some rows have already been extracted from the result set, then it retrieves the remaining rows from the result set.
- **rowcount:** This is a read-only attribute and returns the number of rows that were affected by an execute() method.

Example

The following procedure queries all the records from EMPLOYEE table having salary more than 1000 −

```
import MySQLdb

# Open database connection
db =
MySQLdb.connect("localhost","testuser","test123",
"TESTDB" )

# prepare a cursor object using cursor() method
cursor = db.cursor()

sql = "SELECT * FROM EMPLOYEE \
       WHERE INCOME > '%d'" % (1000)
```

```
try:
    # Execute the SQL command
    cursor.execute(sql)
    # Fetch all the rows in a list of lists.
    results = cursor.fetchall()
    for row in results:
        fname = row[0]
        lname = row[1]
        age = row[2]
        sex = row[3]
        income = row[4]
        # Now print fetched result
        print
"fname=%s,lname=%s,age=%d,sex=%s,income=%d" % \
            (fname, lname, age, sex, income )
except:
    print "Error: unable to fecth data"

# disconnect from server
db.close()
```

This will produce the following result −

```
fname=Mac,      lname=Mohan,       age=20,       sex=M,
income=2000
```

Update Operation

UPDATE Operation on any database means to update one or more records, which are already available in the database.

The following procedure updates all the records having SEX as **'M'**. Here, we increase AGE of all the males by one year.

Example

```
import MySQLdb

# Open database connection
db =
MySQLdb.connect("localhost","testuser","test123",
"TESTDB" )
```

```
# prepare a cursor object using cursor() method
cursor = db.cursor()

# Prepare SQL query to UPDATE required records
sql = "UPDATE EMPLOYEE SET AGE = AGE + 1
                          WHERE SEX = '%c'" %
('M')
try:
    # Execute the SQL command
    cursor.execute(sql)
    # Commit your changes in the database
    db.commit()
except:
    # Rollback in case there is any error
    db.rollback()

# disconnect from server
db.close()
```

DELETE Operation

DELETE operation is required when you want to delete some records from your database. Following is the procedure to delete all the records from EMPLOYEE where AGE is more than 20 –

Example

```
import MySQLdb

# Open database connection
db =
MySQLdb.connect("localhost","testuser","test123",
"TESTDB" )

# prepare a cursor object using cursor() method
cursor = db.cursor()

# Prepare SQL query to DELETE required records
sql = "DELETE FROM EMPLOYEE WHERE AGE > '%d'" %
(20)
try:
```

```
    # Execute the SQL command
    cursor.execute(sql)
    # Commit your changes in the database
    db.commit()
except:
    # Rollback in case there is any error
    db.rollback()

# disconnect from server
db.close()
```

Performing Transactions

Transactions are a mechanism that ensures data consistency. Transactions have the following four properties:

- **Atomicity:** Either a transaction completes or nothing happens at all.
- **Consistency:** A transaction must start in a consistent state and leave the system in a consistent state.
- **Isolation:** Intermediate results of a transaction are not visible outside the current transaction.
- **Durability:** Once a transaction was committed, the effects are persistent, even after a system failure.

The Python DB API 2.0 provides two methods to either *commit* or *rollback* a transaction.

Example

```
# Prepare SQL query to DELETE required records
sql = "DELETE FROM EMPLOYEE WHERE AGE > '%d'" %
(20)
try:
    # Execute the SQL command
    cursor.execute(sql)
    # Commit your changes in the database
```

```
    db.commit()
except:
    # Rollback in case there is any error
    db.rollback()
```

COMMIT Operation

Commit is the operation, which gives a green signal to database to finalize the changes, and after this operation, no change can be reverted back.

Here is a simple example to call **commit** method.

```
db.commit()
```

ROLLBACK Operation

If you are not satisfied with one or more of the changes and you want to revert back those changes completely, then use **rollback()** method.

Here is a simple example to call **rollback()** method.

```
db.rollback()
```

Disconnecting Database

To disconnect Database connection, use close() method.

```
db.close()
```

If the connection to a database is closed by the user with the close() method, any outstanding transactions are rolled back by the DB. However, instead of depending on any of DB lower level implementation details, your application would be better off calling commit or rollback explicitly.

Handling Errors

There are many sources of errors. A few examples are a syntax error in an executed SQL statement, a connection failure, or calling the fetch method for an already canceled or finished statement handle.

The DB API defines a number of errors that must exist in each database module. The following table lists these exceptions.

Exception	Description
Warning	Used for non-fatal issues. Must subclass StandardError.
Error	Base class for errors. Must subclass StandardError.
InterfaceError	Used for errors in the database module, not the database itself. Must subclass Error.
DatabaseError	Used for errors in the database. Must subclass Error.
DataError	Subclass of DatabaseError that refers to errors in the data.
OperationalError	Subclass of DatabaseError that refers to errors such as the loss of a connection to the database. These errors are generally outside of the control of the Python scripter.
IntegrityError	Subclass of DatabaseError for situations that would damage the relational integrity, such as uniqueness constraints or foreign keys.
InternalError	Subclass of DatabaseError that refers to errors internal to the database module, such as a cursor no longer being active.
ProgrammingError	Subclass of DatabaseError that refers to errors such as a bad table name and other things that can safely be blamed on you.
NotSupportedError	Subclass of DatabaseError that refers to trying to call unsupported functionality.

Your Python scripts should handle these errors, but before using any of the above exceptions, make sure your MySQLdb has support for that exception. You can get more information about them by reading the DB API 2.0 specification.

PRACTICAL EXERCISE

1. Write a Python program to print the following string in a specific format (see the output).

Sample String : "Twinkle, twinkle, little star, How I wonder what you are! Up above the world so high, Like a diamond in the sky. Twinkle, twinkle, little star, How I wonder what you are" *Output :*

Twinkle, twinkle, little star,

   How I wonder what you are!

      Up above the world so high,

      Like a diamond in the sky.

Twinkle, twinkle, little star,

   How I wonder what you are

2. Write a Python program to get the Python version you are using.

3. Write a Python program to display the current date and time.
Sample Output :
Current date and time :

2014-07-05 14:34:14

4. Write a Python program which accepts the radius of a circle from the user and compute the area.
Sample Output :
r = 1.1
Area = 3.8013271108436504

5. Write a Python program which accepts the user's first and last name and print them in reverse order with a space between them.

6. Write a Python program which accepts a sequence of comma-separated numbers from user and generate a list and a tuple with those numbers.
Sample data : 3, 5, 7, 23
Output :
List : ['3', ' 5', ' 7', ' 23']
Tuple : ('3', ' 5', ' 7', ' 23')

7. Write a Python program to accept a filename from the user and print the extension of that.
Sample filename : abc.java
Output : java

8. Write a Python program to display the first and last colors from the following list.
color_list = ["Red","Green","White" ,"Black"]

9. Write a Python program to display the examination schedule. (extract the date from exam_st_date).
exam_st_date = (11, 12, 2014)
Sample Output : The examination will start from : 11 / 12 / 2014

10. Write a Python program that accepts an integer (n) and computes the value of n+nn+nnn.
Sample value of n is 5
Expected Result : 615

11. Write a Python program to print the documents (syntax, description etc.) of Python built-in function(s).
Sample function : abs()
Expected Result :
abs(number) -> number
Return the absolute value of the argument.

12. Write a Python program to print the calendar of a given month and year.
Note : Use 'calendar' module.

13. Write a Python program to print the following here document.
Sample string :
a string that you "don't" have to escape
This
is a .... multi-line
heredoc string --------> example

14. Write a Python program to calculate number of days between two dates.
Sample dates : (2014, 7, 2), (2014, 7, 11)
Expected output : 9 days

15. Write a Python program to get the volume of a sphere with radius 6.

16. Write a Python program to get the difference between a given number and 17, if the number is greater than 17 return double the

absolute difference.

17. Write a Python program to test whether a number is within 100 of 1000 or 2000.

18. Write a Python program to calculate the sum of three given numbers, if the values are equal then return thrice of their sum.

19. Write a Python program to get a new string from a given string where "Is" has been added to the front. If the given string already begins with "Is" then return the string unchanged.

20. Write a Python program to get a string which is n (non-negative integer) copies of a given string.

21. Write a Python program to find whether a given number (accept from the user) is even or odd, print out an appropriate message to the user.

22. Write a Python program to count the number 4 in a given list.

23. Write a Python program to get the n (non-negative integer) copies of the first 2 characters of a given string. Return the n copies of the whole string if the length is less than 2.

24. Write a Python program to test whether a passed letter is a vowel or not.

25. Write a Python program to check whether a specified value is contained in a group of values.

Test Data :
3 -> [1, 5, 8, 3] : True
-1 -> [1, 5, 8, 3] : False

26. Write a Python program to create a histogram from a given list of integers.

27. Write a Python program to concatenate all elements in a list into a string and return it.

28. Write a Python program to print all even numbers from a given numbers list in the same order and stop the printing if any numbers that come after 237 in the sequence.
Sample numbers list :

numbers = [

  386, 462, 47, 418, 907, 344, 236, 375, 823, 566, 597, 978, 328, 615, 953, 345,

  399, 162, 758, 219, 918, 237, 412, 566, 826, 248, 866, 950, 626, 949, 687, 217,

  815, 67, 104, 58, 512, 24, 892, 894, 767, 553, 81, 379, 843, 831, 445, 742, 717,

  958,743, 527

  ]

29. Write a Python program to print out a set containing all the colors from color_list_1 which are not present in color_list_2.
Test Data :

```
color_list_1 = set(["White", "Black", "Red"])
color_list_2 = set(["Red", "Green"])
```
Expected Output :
{'Black', 'White'}

30. Write a Python program that will accept the base and height of a triangle and compute the area.

31. Write a Python program to compute the greatest common divisor (GCD) of two positive integers.

32. Write a Python program to get the least common multiple (LCM) of two positive integers.

33. Write a Python program to sum of three given integers. However, if two values are equal sum will be zero.

34. Write a Python program to sum of two given integers. However, if the sum is between 15 to 20 it will return 20.

35. Write a Python program that will return true if the two given integer values are equal or their sum or difference is 5.

36. Write a Python program to add two objects if both objects are an integer type.

37. Write a Python program to display your details like name, age, address in three different lines.

38. Write a Python program to solve (x + y) * (x + y).
Test Data : x = 4, y = 3
Expected Output : (4 + 3) ^ 2) = 49

39. Write a Python program to compute the future value of a specified principal amount, rate of interest, and a number of years.
Test Data : amt = 10000, int = 3.5, years = 7
Expected Output : 12722.79

40. Write a Python program to compute the distance between the points (x1, y1) and (x2, y2).

41. Write a Python program to check whether a file exists.

42. Write a Python program to determine if a Python shell is executing in 32bit or 64bit mode on OS.

43. Write a Python program to get OS name, platform and release information.

44. Write a Python program to locate Python site-packages.

45. Write a python program to call an external command in Python.

46. Write a python program to get the path and name of the file that is currently executing.

47. Write a Python program to find out the number of CPUs using.

48. Write a Python program to parse a string to Float or Integer.

49. Write a Python program to list all files in a directory in Python.

50. Write a Python program to print without newline or space.

51. Write a Python program to determine profiling of Python programs.
Note: A profile is a set of statistics that describes how often and for how long various parts of the program executed. These statistics can be formatted into reports via the pstats module.

52. Write a Python program to print to stderr.

53. Write a python program to access environment variables.

54. Write a Python program to get the current username

55. Write a Python to find local IP addresses using Python's stdlib

56. Write a Python program to get height and width of the console window.

57. Write a program to get execution time for a Python method.

58. Write a python program to sum of the first n positive integers.

59. Write a Python program to convert height (in feet and inches) to centimeters.

60. Write a Python program to calculate the hypotenuse of a right angled triangle.

61. Write a Python program to convert the distance (in feet) to inches, yards, and miles.

62. Write a Python program to convert all units of time into seconds.

63. Write a Python program to get an absolute file path.

64. Write a Python program to get file creation and modification date/times.

65. Write a Python program to convert seconds to day, hour, minutes and seconds.

66. Write a Python program to calculate body mass index.

67. Write a Python program to convert pressure in kilopascals to pounds per square inch, a millimeter of mercury (mmHg) and atmosphere pressure.

68. Write a Python program to calculate the sum of the digits in an integer.

69. Write a Python program to sort three integers without using conditional statements and loops.

70. Write a Python program to sort files by date.

71. Write a Python program to get a directory listing, sorted by creation date.

72. Write a Python program to get the details of math module.

73. Write a Python program to calculate midpoints of a line.

74. Write a Python program to hash a word.

75. Write a Python program to get the copyright information.

76. Write a Python program to get the command-line arguments (name of the script, the number of arguments, arguments) passed to a script.

77. Write a Python program to test whether the system is a big-endian platform or little-endian platform.

78. Write a Python program to find the available built-in modules.

79. Write a Python program to get the size of an object in bytes.

80. Write a Python program to get the current value of the recursion limit.

81. Write a Python program to concatenate N strings.

82. Write a Python program to calculate the sum over a container.

83. Write a Python program to test if a certain number is greater than all numbers of a list.

84. Write a Python program to count the number occurrence of a specific character in a string.

85. Write a Python program to check if a file path is a file or a directory.

86. Write a Python program to get the ASCII value of a character.

87. Write a Python program to get the size of a file.

88. Given variables x=30 and y=20, write a Python program to print t "30+20=50".

89. Write a Python program to perform an action if a condition is true.
Given a variable name, if the value is 1, display the string "First day of a Month!" and do nothing if the value is not equal.

90. Write a Python program to create a copy of its own source code.

91. Write a Python program to swap two variables.

92. Write a Python program to define a string containing special characters in various forms.

93. Write a Python program to get the identity of an object.

94. Write a Python program to convert a byte string to a list of integers.

95. Write a Python program to check if a string is numeric.

96. Write a Python program to print the current call stack.

97. Write a Python program to list the special variables used within the language.

98. Write a Python program to get the system time.

Note : The system time is important for debugging, network information, random number seeds, or something as simple as program performance.

99. Write a Python program to clear the screen or terminal.

100. Write a Python program to get the name of the host on which the routine is running.

101. Write a Python program to access and print a URL's content to the console.

102. Write a Python program to get system command output.

103. Write a Python program to extract the filename from a given path.

104. Write a Python program to get the effective group id, effective user id, real group id, a list of supplemental group ids associated with the current process.
Note: Availability: Unix.

105. Write a Python program to get the users environment.

106. Write a Python program to divide a path on the extension separator.

107. Write a Python program to retrieve file properties.

108. Write a Python program to find path refers to a file or directory when you encounter a path name.

109. Write a Python program to check if a number is positive, negative or zero.

110. Write a Python program to get numbers divisible by fifteen from a list using an anonymous function.

111. Write a Python program to make file lists from current directory using a wildcard.

112. Write a Python program to remove the first item from a specified list.

113. Write a Python program to input a number, if it is not a number generate an error message.

114. Write a Python program to filter the positive numbers from a list.

115. Write a Python program to compute the product of a list of integers (without using for loop).

116. Write a Python program to print Unicode characters.

117. Write a Python program to prove that two string variables of same value point same memory location.

118. Write a Python program to create a bytearray from a list.

119. Write a Python program to display a floating number in specified numbers.

120. Write a Python program to format a specified string to limit the number of characters to 6.

121. Write a Python program to determine if variable is defined or not.

122. Write a Python program to empty a variable without destroying it.

Sample data: n=20
d = {"x":200}
Expected Output : 0
{}

123. Write a Python program to determine the largest and smallest integers, longs, floats.

124. Write a Python program to check if multiple variables have the same value.

125. Write a Python program to sum of all counts in a collections?

126. Write a Python program to get the actual module object for a given object.

127. Write a Python program to check if an integer fits in 64 bits.

128. Write a Python program to check if lowercase letters exist in a string.

129. Write a Python program to add leading zeroes to a string.

130. Write a Python program to use double quotes to display strings.

131. Write a Python program to split a variable length string into variables.

132. Write a Python program to list home directory without absolute path.

133. Write a Python program to calculate the time runs (difference between start and current time) of a program.

134. Write a Python program to input two integers in a single line.

135. Write a Python program to print a variable without spaces between values.
Sample value : x =30
Expected output : Value of x is "30"

136. Write a Python program to find files and skip directories of a given directory.

137. Write a Python program to extract single key-value pair of a dictionary in variables.

138. Write a Python program to convert true to 1 and false to 0.

139. Write a Python program to valid a IP address.

140. Write a Python program to convert an integer to binary keep leading zeros.
Sample data : 50
Expected output : 00001100, 0000001100

141. Write a python program to convert decimal to hexadecimal.
Sample decimal number: 30, 4
Expected output: 1e, 04

142. Write a Python program to find the operating system name, platform and platform release date.
Operating system name:
posix
Platform name:
Linux
Platform release:
4.4.0-47-generic

143. Write a Python program to determine if the python shell is executing in 32bit or 64bit mode on operating system.

144. Write a Python program to check if variable is of integer or string.

145. Write a Python program to find the operating system name, platform and platform release date.
Operating system name:
posix
Platform name:
Linux
Platform release:

4.4.0-47-generic

146. Write a Python program to find the location of Python module sources.
Operating system name:
posix
Platform name:
Linux
Platform release:
4.4.0-47-generic